Mrs. Morgan

Mrs. Morgan's collection of paintings

Mrs. Morgan

Mrs. Morgan's collection of paintings

ISBN/EAN: 9783743304437

Manufactured in Europe, USA, Canada, Australia, Japa

Cover: Foto ©Thomas Meinert / pixelio.de

Manufactured and distributed by brebook publishing software
(www.brebook.com)

Mrs. Morgan

Mrs. Morgan's collection of paintings

Mrs. Morgan's

Collection of Paintings

New-York

1884

Index to Artists' Names

Catalogue

PARLOR

(The first figure shows the width of the picture.)

I

T̲ROYON (C.) dec'd   .   .   .   .   Paris

Pupil of Rivereux.
Medals, 1838–40–46–48–55.
Legion of Honor, 1849.
Born, 1810.   Died, 1865.

RETURN FROM THE FARM.

30 x 19

From the Laurent Richard collection.

2

C̲OROT (J. B. C.) dec'd .   .   .   .   Paris

Pupil of V. Bertin.
Medals, 1838–48–55.
Legion of Honor, 1846.
Medal, Exposition Universelle, 1867.
Officer of the Legion of Honor, 1867.
Diploma to the memory of deceased artists, Exposition Universelle, 1878.
Born, 1796.   Died, 1875.

NYMPHS BATHING.

29 x 39

3

MILLET (J. F.) dec'd . . . . Paris

Pupil of P. Delaroche.
Medals, 1853-64.
Medal, Exposition Universelle, 1867.
Legion of Honor, 1868.
Diploma to the memory of deceased artists, Exposition Universelle,
1878.
Born, 1814. Died, 1875.

WOMAN IN KITCHEN.

3 x 4½

4

KNAUS (L.) . . . . Berlin

Pupil of the Düsseldorf Academy.
Medals, 1853-57-59.
Medal, Exposition Universelle, 1855.
Legion of Honor, 1859.
Grand Medal of Honor, Exposition Universelle, 1867.
Officer of the Legion of Honor, 1867.
Medal, Vienna, 1882.
Medal, Munich, 1883.
Professor in the Academy, Berlin.
Member of the Academies of Berlin, Vienna, Munich, Amsterdam,
Antwerp, and Christiana.
Knight of the Order of Merit.
Medals at Berlin, Weimar, Munich, &c.

THE HUNTER'S REPAST.

19 x 24

BONNAT (Leon) . . . . . Paris

Pupil of Cogniet.
Medals, 1861–63–67.
Legion of Honor, 1867.
Medal of Honor, 1869.
Officer of the Legion of Honor, 1874.
Member of the Institute of France, 1881.
Knight of the Order of Leopold, 1881.
Commander of the Legion of Honor, 1882.

AN ARAB CHIEF.

27 x 23

VAN MARCKE (E.) . . . . Paris

Pupil of Troyon.
Medals, 1867–69–70.
Legion of Honor, 1872.
First Class Medal, Exposition Universelle, 1878.

COWS DRINKING.

19 x 13

TADEMA-ALMA (L.) R. A. . . London

Pupil of Leys.
Member of the Royal Academy, Amsterdam, 1863.
Medal at the Salon, Paris, 1864.
Knight of the Order of Leopold (Belgium), 1866.
Second Class Medal at the Exposition Universelle, Paris, 1867.
Knight of the Order of the Dutch Lion, 1868.
Knight, First Class, of the Order of Merit of St. Michael, Bavaria,
1869.
Member of the Royal Academy of Munich, 1871.
Knight of the Order of the Legion d'Honneur, France, 1873.
Grand Gold Medal, Berlin, 1874.
Member of the Royal Academy of Berlin, 1875.
Member of the Society of Painters in Water-colors, London.
Knight of the Third Class, Lion d'Or of the House of Nassau,
1876.
Knight of the Third Class of the Kœnigliche Kronen-Orden of
Prussia, 1877.
Honorary Professor of the Royal Institute of Fine Arts, Naples,
1878.
First Class Medal at the Exposition Universelle, Paris, 1878.
Officer of the Legion of Honor, 1878.
Member of the Royal Academy, London.

SPRING.

When Winter's rage abates, when cheerful hours
Awake the Spring and Spring awakes the flowers,
On the green turf they careless limbs display,
And celebrate the mighty mother's day;
For then the hills with pleasing shades are crown'd
And sleeps are sweeter on the silken ground;
With milder beams the sun securely shines.

Fat are the lambs and luscious are the wines,
Let every swain adore her power divine,
And milk and honey mix with sparkling wine;
Let all the choir of clowns attend the show,
In long procession, shouting as they go;
Invoking her to bless their yearly stores,
Inviting plenty to their crowded floors.

Thus in the Spring, and thus in Summer's heat,
Before the sickles touch the ripening wheat,
On Ceres' call; and let the labouring hind
With oaken wreaths his hollow temples bind;
On Ceres let him call, and Ceres praise,
With uncouth dances and with country lays.

(*Georgics — Translated by John Dryden.*)

21 x 35

S

VIBERT (J. G.) . . . . . . Paris

Pupil of Barrias.
Medals, 1864-67-68.
Legion of Honor, 1870.
Third Class Medal, Exposition Universelle, 1878.

THE CARDINALS' MENU.

28 x 22

9

ROUSSEAU (Theo.) dec'd . . . . Paris

Pupil of Lethiere.
Medals, 1834-49-55.
Legion of Honor, 1852.
One of the eight Grand Medals of Honor, Exposition Universelle,
1867.
Diploma to the memory of deceased artists, Exposition Universelle,
1878.
Born, 1812. Died, 1867.

A MOUND, "JEAN DE PARIS."

*AUTUMN IN THE FOREST OF FONTAINE-
BLEAU.*

20 x 25

(From the collections of Baron Crabbe, Didier, and Laurent
Richard.)

10

SCHREYER (Ad.) . . . . . . Paris

Medals, 1864-65, Medal, Exposition Universelle, 1867.
Vienna Exposition, 1873.

ARAB AT FOUNTAIN.

2250

II

DELACROIX (Eugene) dec'd   .   .   **Paris**

Pupil of Guérin.
Medals, 1824-48.
Legion of Honor, 1831.
Officer of the Legion of Honor, 1846.
Commander of the Legion of Honor, 1855.
Medal of Honor, Exposition Universelle, 1855.
Member of the Institute of France, 1857.
Born, 1798.   Died, 1863.

TIGER AND SERPENT.

16 x 12

12

BOUGUEREAU (W. A.)   .   .   .   **Paris**

Pupil of Picot.
Prize of Rome, 1850.
Medal, 1857.   Medal, Exposition Universelle, 1855.
Legion of Honor, 1859.
Medal, Exposition Universelle, 1867.
Member of the Institute of France, 1876.
Officer of the Legion of Honor, 1876.
Medal of Honor, Exposition Universelle, 1878.
Knight of the Order of Leopold, 1881.

CUPID.

22 x 25

13

MEISSONIER (J. L. E.) . . . **Paris**

Pupil of Cogniet
Medals, 1840-41-43-48.
Legion of Honor, 1846.
Grand Medal of Honor, Exposition Universelle, 1855.
Officer of the Legion of Honor, 1856.
Member of the Institute of France, 1861.
Honorary Member of the Royal Academy, London.
One of the eight Grand Medals of Honor, Exposition Universelle,
1867.
Commander of the Legion of Honor, 1867.
Grand Medal of Honor, Exposition Universelle, 1878.
Grand Officer of the Legion of Honor, 1881.

A STANDARD BEARER.

10 x 14

14

DECAMPS (A. G.) dec'd . . . Paris

Pupil of Pujol.
Medals, 1831-34.
Chevalier of the Legion of Honor, 1839.
Officer of the Legion of Honor, 1851.
Born, 1803.   Died, 1860.

BAZAARS IN CAIRO.

9 x 11

15

PASINI (A.) . . . . . . Paris

Pupil of Ciceri.
Medals, 1859-63-64.
Legion of Honor, 1868.
Grand Medal of Honor, Exposition Universelle, 1878.
Officer of the Legion of Honor, 1878.

COURT-YARD IN CONSTANTINOPLE.

7 x 9

11   250

MEYER VON BREMEN (J. G.) . Berlin

Pupil of Sohn.
Member of the Amsterdam Academy.
Gold Medal of Prussia, 1850.
Medals at Berlin and Philadelphia.

WOMAN'S HEAD.

6 x 9

17 /2000

BRETON (Jules) . . . . . Paris

Pupil of Devigne and Drolling.
Medals, 1855-57-59-61.
Legion of Honor, 1861.
Medal of the First Class and Officer of the Legion of Honor at the
Exposition Universelle, 1867.
Medal of Honor, Salon, 1872.
Knight of the Order of Leopold, 1881.

COMMUNICANTS.

74 x 48

Exhibited at the Paris Salon, 1884.

TRANSLATION OF A POEM BY JULES BRETON, ILLUSTRATING THIS
PAINTING.

Among the fresh lilacs, and the new budding leaves,
In this spring-time that hums and smiles through the trees,
On this bright Sabbath day, maids with heavenly brows,
Marching onward to mass, beneath the young boughs:
Did you take from the sky, to commune for God's pleasure,
Your robes of pure white where quivers the azure?

Thus so would I think from your costumes so light
That bloom with the day, like the snow and as bright:
By the vapory veil, with its misty-like flounces,
By your virginal lips, and your sweet modest glances;
By your nosegays of gold, attached to your tapers,
And the heavenly light that illumines your faces.

12

How each thing around both greets you and blesses;
The mossy thatched roofs have enameled their ridges;
They curve rounding down to contours most supple;
The soft, tender grass does everywhere sparkle;
Still wet by the morn, its white dew breathing odors,
It unrolls to your feet its velvety borders.

Your folds of gauze in the breeze make angelic pinions,
Less white are the doves on the barn's lofty crestings;
Less pure is the hawthorn, with its balmy branches;
Thus onward you go to the old chapel's porches;
Where girdled by lindens the church bell is tolling,
While the sun on the tower its corners is gilding.

And spotless you go. The portal unfolds,
Your heart stronger beats, the bell louder tolls;
The aged, quite moved, at the tower's base center,
The door opens wide. Go, gentle maids, enter;
And then from the burning ends of your nun's tapers,
Let bright stars of love float out with its vapors.

Ecstasy! holy fear of mystical raptures
When with your fingers quiver the hymnal's pages
In singing! O sweet tender Jesus, descend!
Ah! come, Divine Spouse, and with our soul blend.
The Host seems to tremble in the hands of the priest,
As seen through the whirl of the incense's mist.

Receive in his body the Lord of the earth;
Daughters, you ignore his mysterious worth;
And to him prefer, resuscitated being
The beautiful crucifix, on the hill dying;
You love its fair forehead, that's torn by the thorn,
And the bleeding wound on its holy side shown.

And above all, you love the child's rosy face,
Bathed, as the fair lamb, in the gold of its fleece;
Who came with its smiles, at the side of your cribs,
And its little clear eyes, when you were all babes;
'Tis for this that you beam, is it not, maiden, say?
And palpitate in the church aisles while you stay.

Vainly all reason succeeds to dead faith,
And no recollection goes forth with your breath
That does not vibrate like a ray from the skies,
So sing, virgins, sing! The glad summer close lies;
Then autumn, whose ripe fruits will fall to the ground;
So to dying spring, let your first chant resound.

FROMENTIN (E.) dec'd . . . Paris

Pupil of Cabat.
Medals, 1849-57-59.
Legion of Honor, 1859.
Medal, Exposition Universelle, 1867.
Officer of the Legion of Honor, 1869.
Diploma to the memory of deceased artists,
Exposition Universelle, 1878.
Born, 1820. Died, 1876.

ARAB HORSEMEN.

16 x 12

19

ROUSSEAU (Theo.) dec'd . . . Paris

Pupil of Lethiere.
Medals, 1834-47-55.
Legion of Honor, 1852.
One of the eight Grand Medals of Honor, Exposition Universelle,
1867.
Diploma to the memory of deceased artists, Exposition Universelle,
1878. Born, 1812. Died, 1867.

LANDSCAPE AND **COTTAGES.**

12 x 8   *3500*

20

DIAZ (N.) dec'd . . . . . Paris

Medals, 1844-46-48.
Legion of Honor, 1851.
Diploma to the memory of deceased artists,
Exposition Universelle, 1878.
Born, 1807. Died, 1876.

THE BATHERS.   *1500*

16 x 10

21

MEISSONIER (J. L. E.) . . . **Paris**

Pupil of Cogniet.
Medals, 1840–41–43–48.
Legion of Honor, 1846.
Grand Medal of Honor, Exposition Universelle, 1855.
Officer of the Legion of Honor, 1856.
Member of the Institute of France, 1861.
Honorary Member of the Royal Academy, London.
One of the eight Grand Medals of Honor, Exposition Universelle, 1867.
Commander of the Legion of Honor, 1867.
Grand Medal of Honor, Exposition Universelle, 1878.
Grand officer of the Legion of Honor, 1881.

IN THE LIBRARY.

12 x 18

22

MILLET (J. F.) dec'd . . . . **Paris**

Pupil of P. Delaroche.
Medals, 1853–64.
Medal, Exposition Universelle, 1867.
Legion of Honor, 1868.
Diploma to the memory of deceased artists, Exposition Universelle,
1878.
Born, 1814. Died, 1875.

GATHERING BEANS.

(Millet's mother and the cottage where he was born.)

12 x 15

23

MEYER VON BREMEN (J. G.) . **Berlin**

Pupil of Sohn.
Member of the Amsterdam Academy.
Gold Medal of Prussia, 1850.
Medals at Berlin and Philadelphia.

BREAD AND MILK.

9 x 11

DOMINGO (J.) . . . . . . Paris

CARD PLAYERS.

4 × 5   *12.50*

25

BONHEUR (Rosa, Mlle.) . . . . Paris

Pupil of her father.
Medals, 1845-48.
Medal, Exposition Universelle, 1855.
Legion of Honor, 1865.
Medal, Exposition Universelle, 1867.

COW AND CALF.

SCOTCH HIGHLANDS.

32 x 25   *1000*

26

DIAZ (N.) dec'd . . . . . . Paris

Medals, 1844-46-48.
Legion of Honor, 1851.
Diploma to the memory of deceased artists, Exposition Universelle,
1878.
Born, 1807.   Died, 1876.

CHILDREN PLAYING WITH A KID.

18 x 22   *2000*

SEITS (Antoine) . . . . Munich

Pupil of the Munich Academy.
Professor and Honorary Member of the Royal Academy
of Munich.
Gold Medal at Munich.
Gold Medal at Vienna.
Chevalier of the Bavarian Order of St. Michael, etc.

*MOTHER **AND** INFANT.*

6 x 8   *4 50*

28

COROT (J. B. C.) dec'd . . . **Paris**

Pupil of V. Bertin.
Medals, 1838–48–55.
Legion of Honor, 1846.
Medal, Exposition Universelle, 1867.
Officer of the Legion of Honor, 1867.
Diploma to the memory of deceased artists, Exposition Universelle,
1878.
Born, 1796. Died, 1875.

WOOD GATHERERS.   *7500*

63 x 44

29

MEYER VON BREMEN (J. G.) . **Berlin**

Pupil of Sohn.
Member of the Amsterdam Academy.
Gold Medal of Prussia, 1840.
Medals at Berlin and Philadelphia.

THE WONDER BOOK.

6 x 7   *500*

DIAZ (N.) dec'd . . . . . **Paris**

Medals, 1844–46–48.
Legion of Honor, 1851.
Diploma to the memory of deceased artists, Exposition Universelle,
1878.
Born, 1807. Died, 1876.

HOLY FAMILY.

20 x 27

31

WORMS (Jules) . . . . . Paris

Pupil of Lafosse.
Medals, 1867–68–69.
Legion of Honor, 1876.
Medal, Exposition Universelle, 1878.

SPANISH MARKET-DAY.

31 x 24

32

SCHREYER (Ad.) . . . . . Paris

Medals, 1864–65.
Medal, Exposition Universelle, 1867.
Vienna Exposition, 1873.

WALLACHIAN POST STATION.

6 x 8

33

WILLEMS (F.) . . . . . Paris

Medals, 1844–46–55.
Medal at Brussels, 1843.
Chevalier of the Order of Leopold.
Legion of Honor, 1853.
Officer of the Order of Leopold, 1855.
Officer of the Legion of Honor, 1864.
Medal, Exposition Universelle, 1867.
First Class Medal, Exposition Universelle, 1878.

THE MUSIC LESSON.

27 x 39   2000.

34

BOUGUEREAU (W. A.) . . . Paris

Pupil of Picot.
Prize of Rome, 1850.
Medal, 1857.
Medal, Exposition Universelle, 1855.
Legion of Honor, 1859.
Medal, Exposition Universelle, 1867.
Member of the Institute of France, 1876.
Officer of the Legion of Honor, 1876.
Medal of Honor, Exposition Universelle, 1878.
Knight of the Order of Leopold, 1881.

ITALIAN MOTHER AND CHILD.

17 x 22   1500

35

TROYON (C.) dec'd . . . . Paris

Pupil of Rivereaux.
Medals, 1838–40–46–55.
Legion of Honor, 1849.
Born, 1810. Died, 1865.

GOING TO THE FAIR.

34 x 24   2500

36

DE NEUVILLE (A.) . . . . Paris

Pupil of Picot.
Medals, 1859–61.
Legion of Honor, 1873.
Officer of the Legion of Honor, 1881.

FRENCH CUIRASSIER.

19 x 23

37

BELLECOUR (Berne) . . . . **Paris**

Pupil of Picot.
Medals, 1869–72.
Medal, Exposition Universelle, 1878.

THE PRISONER.

25 x 39

38

STEVENS (Alfred) . . . . **Paris**

Gold Medal at Brussels, 1851.
Paris, 1853.
Medal, Exposition Universelle, 1855.
Legion of Honor, 1863.
Officer of the Legion of Honor, 1867.
Commander of the Order of Leopold.
First Class Medal, Exposition Universelle, 1878.
Grand Officer of the Order of Leopold, 1881.
Officer of the Order of St. Michel of Bavaria.

CONVERSATION.

20 x 29

20

CABANEL (A.) . . . . . **Paris**

Pupil of Picot.
Prize of Rome, 1845.
Medal, 1852.
Medal, Exposition Universelle, 1855.
Legion of Honor, 1855.
Member of the Institute of France, 1863.
Officer of the Legion of Honor, 1864.
Grand Medal of Honor, 1865.
Medal, Exposition Universelle, 1867.
Commander of the Legion of Honor, 1878.
Grand Medal of Honor, Exposition Universelle, 1878.
Professor in the School of the Beaux Arts.

DESDEMONA.

17 x 21

40

COROT (J. B. C.) dec'd . . . . Paris

Pupil of V. Bertin.
Medals, 1838–48.
Legion of Honor, 1846.
Medal, Exposition Universelle, 1855.
Officer of the Legion of Honor, 1867.
Diploma to the memory of deceased artists, Exposition Universelle, 1878.
Born, 1796. Died, 1875.

LANDSCAPE AND CATTLE.

23 x 15

41

DUPRÉ (Jules) . . . . . Paris

Medal, 1833.
Legion of Honor, 1849.
Medal, Exposition Universelle, 1867.
Officer of the Legion of Honor, 1870.

A CLOUDY DAY.

14 x 18

3

MARIS (M.) . . . . . Hague

THE TRYSTING PLACE.

17 x 13 *1200*

BOUGUEREAU (W. A.) . . . Paris

Pupil of Picot.
Prize of Rome, 1850.
Medal, 1857.
Medal, Exposition Universelle, 1855.
Legion of Honor, 1859.
Medal, Exposition Universelle, 1867.
Member of the Institute of France, 1876.
Officer of the Legion of Honor, 1876.
Medal of Honor, Exposition Universelle, 1878.
Knight of the Order of Leopold, 1881.

NUT GATHERERS.

52 x 34 *2500*

MILLET (J. F.) dec'd . . . . Paris

Pupil of P. Delaroche.
Medals, 1853-64.
Medal, Exposition Universelle, 1867.
Legion of Honor, 1868.
Diploma to the memory of deceased artists, Exposition
Universelle, 1878.
Born, 1814. Died, 1875.

THE SPADERS.

38 x 30 *3300*

VAN MARCKE (E.) . . . . Paris

Pupil of Troyon.
Medals, 1867-69-70.
Legion of Honor, 1872.
First Class Medal Exposition Universelle, 1878.

COWS IN A POOL. 750

24 x 19

46

GÉRÔME (J. L.) . . . . . Paris

Pupil of P. Delaroche.
Medals, 1847-48.
Medal, Exposition Universelle, 1855.
Legion of Honor, 1855.
Member of the Institute of France, 1865.
Honorary Member of the Royal Academy, London.
One of the eight Grand Medals of Honor, Exposition Universelle, 1867.
Officer of the Legion of Honor, 1867.
Grand Medal of Honor, 1874.
Commander of the Legion of Honor, 1878.
Medal, Sculpture, Exposition Universelle, 1878.
Grand Medal of Honor, Exposition Universelle, 1878.
Professor in the School of the Beaux Arts.

VASE SELLER — CAIRO. 2500

14 x 18

47

DIAZ (N.) dec'd . . . . . Paris

Medals, 1844-46-48.
Legion of Honor, 1851.
Diploma to the memory of deceased artists, Exposition Universelle, 1878.
Born, 1807. Died, 1876.

EDGE OF A WOOD. 900

16 x 12

DOMINGO (J.) . . . . . Paris

HEAD OF A SPANISH CAVALIER.

6 x 8

49

MONTICELLI. . . . . . Paris

ADORATION OF THE MAGI.

25 x 13

50

MILLET (J. F.) dec'd . . . . Paris

Pupil of P. Delaroche.
Medals, 1853-64.
Medal, Exposition Universelle, **1867.**
Legion of Honor, 1868.
Diploma to the memory of deceased artists, Exposition
Universelle, 1878.
Born, 1814. Died, 1875.

THE *SPINNER.*

28 x 36

51

NICOL (Erskine) A. R. A.   . .   London

Pupil of the Trustees' Academy, Edinburgh.
Medal, Exposition Universelle, 1867.
Member of the Royal Scottish Academy.
Member of the Royal Academy, London.

PILLS FOR THE SAXON.

27 x 19   *1000*

52

MILLET (J. F.) dec'd . . . . Paris

Pupil of P. Delaroche.
Medals, 1853-64.
Medal, Exposition Universelle, 1867.
Legion of Honor, 1868.
Diploma to the memory of deceased artists, Exposition Universelle, 1878.
Born, 1814. Died, 1875.

DRESSING FLAX.

17 x 21   *5000*

53

DIAZ (N.) **dec'd** . . . . . Paris

Medals, 1844-46-48.
Legion of Honor, 1851.
Diploma to the memory of deceased artists, Exposition Universelle,
1878.
Born, 1807. Died, 1876.

LANE NEAR FONTAINEBLEAU

25 x 19

1 0 00

54

KNIGHT (D. R.) . . . . . . Paris

Pupil of Gleyre and Meissonier.

NOONDAY REPAST.

25 x 20

5 00

55

GÉRÔME (J. L.) . . . . . Paris

Pupil of P. Delaroche.
Medals, 1847-48.
Medal, Exposition Universelle, 1855.
Legion of Honor, 1855.
Member of the Institute of France, 1865.
Honorary Member of the Royal Academy, London.
One of the eight Grand Medals of Honor, Exposition Universelle, 1867.
Officer of the Legion of Honor, 1867.
Grand Medal of Honor, 1874.
Commander of the Legion of Honor, 1878
Medal, Sculpture, Exposition Universelle, 1878.
Grand Medal of Honor, Exposition Universelle, 1878.
Professor in the School of the Beaux Arts.

COFFEE-HOUSE, CAIRO.

Bashi-Bazouks casting balls.

26 x 21

45 00

MILLET (J. F.) dec'd . . . . Paris

Pupil of P. Delaroche.
Medals, 1853–64.
Medal, Exposition Universelle, 1867.
Legion of Honor, 1868.
Diploma to the memory of deceased artists, Exposition Universelle,
1878.
Born, 1814. Died, 1875.

SHEPHERDESS AND SHEEP.

Water-color.

10 x 15

NEUHUYS (A.) . . . . . . Hague

THE READING LESSON.

13 x 18

BONVIN (François S.) . . . . Paris

Medals, 1849–51.
Legion of Honor, 1870.

A PINCH OF SNUFF.

13 x 20

WORMS (Jules) . . . . . Paris

Pupil of Lafosse.
Medals, 1867-68-69.
Legion of Honor, 1876.
Medal, Exposition Universelle, 1878.

600

THE PROPOSAL.

14 x 17

60

CAMERON (Hugh) . . . . London

Member of the Royal Scottish Academy.

CARRYING LITTLE SISTER.

11 x 15

500

61

PIOT (Adolphe) . . . . . Paris

Pupil of Cogniet.

THE YOUNG WANDERER.

34 x 51

500

62

NICOL (Erskine) **A. R. A.** . . London

Pupil of the Trustees' Academy, Edinburgh.
Medal, Exposition Universelle, 1867.
Member of the Royal Scottish Academy.
Member of the Royal Academy, London.

BACHELOR LIFE.

23 x 17

1200

28

63

BLOMMERS (B. J.) . . . . Hague

DEPARTURE OF THE FISHER'S BOAT.

25 x 18   500

64

ZIEM (Felix) . . . . . . Paris

Medals, 1851–52–55.
Legion of Honor, 1857.

FISHING BOATS.   400

Bay of Venice.

31 x 19

65

JIMINEZ Y ARANDA (José) . Seville

GOSSIP.

27 x 19   3000

66

CONSTABLE (John) dec'd . . London

Member of the Royal Academy.
Born, 1776. Died, 1837.

ENGLISH LANDSCAPE.   3000

34 x 26

67

MARIS (M.)   .   .   .   .   Hague

VILLAGE IN HOLLAND.

13 x 10

68

ESCOSURA (Léon y.)   .   .   .   .   Paris

Pupil of Gérôme.
Commander of the Order of Isabel the Catholic.
Chevalier of the Order of Charles III. of Spain.
Chevalier of the Order of Christ, of Portugal.

END OF THE GAME.

6 x 4

69

WORMS (Jules)   .   .   .   .   Paris

Pupil of Lafosse.
Medals, 1867-68-69.
Legion of Honor, 1876.
Medal, Exposition Universelle, 1878.

SPANISH FORTUNE-TELLER.

31 x 23

70

DETAILLE (E.)   .   .   .   .   Paris

Pupil of Meissonier.
Medals, 1869-70-72.
Legion of Honor, 1873.
Officer of the Legion of Honor, 1881.

A FLAG-OFFICER.

14 x 17

30

HOGUET (Charles) dec'd   .   .   .   **Berlin**

Pupil of Isabey.
Member of the Berlin Academy.
Medal, Paris, 1848.
Born, 1821.   Died, 1870.

LANDSCAPE.

5 x 7

7 00

BEYLE (Pierre M.)   .   .   .   Paris

Medal, 1881.

GATHERING MUSSELS.

14 x 21

250

CLAYS (P. J.) .   .   .   .   .   **Brussels**

Medal, Exposition Universelle, 1867.
Legion of Honor, 1875.
Chevalier of the Order of Leopold.
Medal, Exposition Universelle, 1878.

DUTCH SHIPPING.

20 x 25

400

PIOT (Adolphe)   .   .   .   .   Paris

Pupil of Cogniet.

ADORATION.

17 x 21

300

FORTUNY (Mariano) dec'd . . . . Rome

Diploma to the memory of deceased artists, Exposition Universelle,
1878.
Born, 1838. Died, 1874.

ITALIAN WOMAN.

Water-color.

6 x 9

76

KNAUS (L.) . . . . Berlin

Pupil of the Düsseldorf Academy.
Medals, 1853-57-59.
Medal, Exposition Universelle, 1855.
Legion of Honor, 1859.
Grand Medal of Honor, Exposition Universelle, 1867.
Officer of the Legion of Honor, 1867.
Medal, Vienna, 1882.
Medal, Munich, 1883.
Professor in the Academy, Berlin.
Member of the Academies of Berlin, Vienna, Munich, Amsterdam,
Antwerp, and Christiana.
Knight of the Order of Merit.
Medals at Berlin, Weimar, Munich, etc.

A FARMER'S DAUGHTER.

9 x 7

MILLET (J. F.) dec'd . . . . . Paris

Pupil of P. Delaroche.
Medals, 1853–64.
Medal, Exposition Universelle, 1867.
Legion of Honor, 1868.
Diploma to the memory of deceased artists, Exposition Universelle,
1878.
Born, 1814. Died, 1875.

FEEDING POULTRY.   *1750*

14 x 17

COUTURE (Thos.) dec'd . . . **Paris**

Pupil of Gros.
Medals, 1844–47–55.
Legion of Honor, 1848.
Born, 1815. Died, 1878.

FAUST AND MEPHISTOPHELES.

10 x 14   *1500*

COUTURE (Thos.) dec'd . . . Paris

Pupil of Gros.
Medals, 1844–47–55.
Legion of Honor, 1848.
Born, 1815. Died, 1878.

A FRENCH REPUBLICAN, 1795.

14 x 17

80

LE ROUX (Hector) . . . . Paris

Pupil of Picot.
Medals, 1863–64–74
Legion of Honor, 1877.
Medal, Exposition Universelle, 1878.

SLEEPING VESTAL.

27 x 54

81

PERRAULT (Léon) . . . . Paris

Pupil of Bouguereau.
Medals, 1864–76.

A YOUNG GLEANER.

36 x 50

82

MONTICELLI . . . . . Paris

A GARDEN PARTY.

30 x 17

83

BENEDICTER (A.) . . . . Munich

MOTHER AND CHILD.

12 x 15

34

84

LELOIR (Louis) . . . **Paris**

Pupil of his father.
Medals, 1864–68–70.
Legion of Honor, 1876.
Second Class Medal, Exposition Universelle, 1878.
Born, 1843. Died, 1883.

THREE STAGES OF LIFE. *1000*

Water-color design for a Fan.

32 x 11

85

DAUBIGNY (C. F.) dec'd . . **Paris**

Pupil of P. Delaroche.
Medals, 1848–53–55–57–59–67.
Legion of Honor, 1859.
Officer of the Legion of Honor, 1874.
Diploma to the memory of deceased artists, Exposition Universelle,
1878.
Born, 1817. Died, 1878.

BOATS ON THE SHORE.

21 x 12

300

86

KOWALSKI (A. W.) . . . **Munich**

Pupil of Jos. Brandt.

HUNTING.

40 x 31

35 *700*

87

CEDERSTROM (Theo.) . . . Munich

A TIGHT CORK.

7 × 9

/50

88

DUPRÉ (Jules) . . . . . Paris

Medal, 1833.
Legion of Honor, 1849.
Medal, Exposition Universelle, 1867.
Officer of the Legion of Honor, 1870.

STORMY WEATHER.

18 × 21

/250

89

CONRAD (Alb.) . . . . . Munich

A TYROLESE INN.

30 × 36

500

90

LYMAN (Jos., Jr.) . . . . New-York

WAITING FOR THE TIDE.

31 x 36   250

91

LÖEFFTZ (L.) . . . . . Munich

Professor in the Academy of Fine Arts at Munich.

MONEY CHANGERS.

39 x 31   1500

4   37

SCHREYER (Ad.) . . . . . **Paris**

Medals, 1864-65.
Medal, Exposition Universelle, 1867.
Vienna Exposition, 1873.

WALLACHIAN PACK HORSES.

36 x 25   *1 000*

93

BOUGUEREAU (W. A.) . . . Paris

Pupil of Picot.
Prize of Rome, 1850.
Medal, 1857.
Medal, Exposition Universelle, 1855.
Legion of Honor, 1859.
Medal, Exposition Universelle, 1867.
Member of the Institute of France, 1876.
Officer of the Legion of Honor, 1876.
Medal of Honor, Exposition Universelle, 1878.
Knight of the Order of Leopold, 1881.

MADONNA, INFANT SAVIOUR, AND ST.
JOHN.

42 x 74   *6500*

94

BOUCHARD (Louis P.) . . . Paris

Pupil of Lefebvre.

THE PET KID.

28 x 45
38   *250*

95

COROT (J. B. C.) dec'd . . . . Paris

Pupil of V. Bertin.
Medals, 1838-48-55.
Legion of Honor, 1846.
Medal, Exposition Universelle, 1867.
Officer of the Legion of Honor, 1867.
Diploma to the memory of deceased artists, Exposition Universelle,
1878.
Born, 1796. Died, 1875.

3000

LANDSCAPE.

20 x 15

96

MEYER VON BREMEN (J. G.) . Berlin

Pupil of Sohn.
Member of the Amsterdam Academy.
Gold Medal of Prussia, 1850.
Medals at Berlin and Philadelphia.

RETURN FROM THE VINTAGE.

23 x 43

2000

97

BÖEHM (Palik) . . . . Munich

Medal, Vienna, 1882.

WAYSIDE FOUNTAIN — HUNGARY.

47 × 30

3 00

98

BROZIK (Vacslav) . . . . Paris

Pupil of Münkacsy.
Medal, 1878.

THE FALCONER'S RECITAL.

54 × 36

1500

99

VIRY (Paul) . . . . . Paris

Pupil of Picot.

MY LADY'S PAGE.

21 × 17

250

40

100

FROMENTIN (E.) dec'd . . . Paris

Pupil of Cabat.
Medals, 1849-57-59. Exposition Universelle, 1867.
Legion of Honor, 1859.
Officer of the Legion of Honor, 1869.
Diploma to the memory of deceased artists, Exposition Universelle,
1878.
Born, 1820. Died, 1876.

ON THE NILE, NEAR PHILÆ.

43 x 24

101

RYDER (P. P.) . . . . New-York

SHELLING PEAS.

20 x 16

102

JIMINEZ y ARANDA (José) . . Seville

INTERESTING NEWS.

27 x 22

103

VERBOECKHOVEN (E.) dec'd . Brussels

Medals, 1824-41-55.
Legion of Honor, 1845.
Chevalier of the Order of Leopold, St. Michael of Bavaria, and
Christ of Portugal.
Decorated with the Iron Cross.
Member of the Royal Academies of Belgium, Antwerp, and St.
Petersburg.
Born, 1799. Died, 1881.

SHEEP LEAVING THE BARN.

35 x 24

104

HENNER (Jean J.) . . . . Paris

Pupil of Drolling and Picot.
Prize of Rome, 1858.
Medals, 1863-65-66.
Legion of Honor, 1873.
Officer of the Legion of Honor, 1878.
Medal, Exposition Universelle, 1878.

SLEEPING NYMPH.

26 x 16

105

RICHET (Léon) . . . . . Paris

Pupil of Lefebvre.

COMING FROM LABOR.

32 x 24

42

SCHEFFER (Ary) dec'd . . . . **Paris**

Pupil of Guérin.
Grand Prize for Painting at Antwerp, 1816.
Medals, 1824-31.
Legion of Honor, 1837.
Born, 1795. Died, 1858.

CHRIST IN THE GARDEN.

12 x 17 *500*

107

KOEK KOEK (B. C.) dec'd . . Amsterdam

Pupil of Schelfout.
Medals, 1840-43.
Chevalier of the Order of the Lion of Netherlands, and Leopold of
Belgium.
Medals at Amsterdam and the Hague.
Born, 1803. Died, 1862.

WINTER IN HOLLAND.

28 x 23 *1600*

108

PELEZ (Fernand) . . . . . Paris

Pupil of Cabanel.
Medals, 1876-79-80.

WITHOUT A HOME.

26 x 36

250

43

BRIDGMAN (Frederick A.) . . . Paris

Pupil of Gérôme.
Medal, 1877.
Medal, Exposition Universelle, 1878.
Legion of Honor, 1878.

AFTERNOON HOURS—ALGIERS.

36 x 25

110

BAUGNIET (Charles) . . . **Sèvres**

Pupil of Drolling.
Medals, 1865. Vienna, 1873.
Chevalier of the Order of Leopold of Belgium, of Isabel the Catholic,
of Christ of Portugal, and of the Branche Ernestine de Saxe.

THE BRIDE'S TOILET.

18 x 27

III

DELACROIX (Eugene) dec'd . . . Paris

Pupil of Guérin.
Medals, 1824–48.
Legion of Honor, 1831.
Officer of the Legion of Honor, 1846.
Commander of the Legion of Honor, 1855.
Medal of Honor, Exposition Universelle, 1855.
Member of the Institute of France, 1857.
Born, 1798. Died, 1863.

LANDSCAPE.

13 x 8

112

V<small>AN</small> MARCKE (E.) . . . . . Paris

Pupil of Troyon.
Medals, 1867–69–70.
Legion of Honor, 1872.
First Class Medal, Exposition Universelle, 1878.

ON THE CLIFFS. 1500

38 x 28

113

R<small>ENTAL</small> (Max) . . . . . . Munich

Medal, Munich, 1881.

NORWEGIAN FISHER'S DANCE.

41 x 30 250

114

G<small>UNTHER</small> (Otto) dec'd . . . Munich

Professor at the Academy of Königsberg.
Gold Medal, Berlin, 1876
Born, 1838. Died, 1884.

THE PASTOR'S VISIT.

45 x 32 750

115

VIBERT (J. G.) . . . . Paris

Pupil of Barrias.
Medals, 1864–67–68.
Legion of Honor, 1870.
Third Class Medal, Exposition Universelle, 1878.

EYES AND EARS.

12 x 19

116

CASANOVA (Antonio) . . . . Paris

Pupil of Madrazo.

THE GOURMAND.

15 x 19

46

117

DELORT (Chas. E.)   .   .   .   .   Paris

Pupil of Gérôme.
Medals, 1875–82.

150

"*MY NEIGHBOR.*"

8 x 12

118

DELORT (Chas. E.)   .   .   .   .   Paris

Pupil of Gérôme.
Medals, 1875–82.

"*ACROSS THE WAY.*"

200

8 x 12

119

VOLTZ (Fr.) .   .   .   .   .   .   Berlin

Pupil of the Munich Academy.
Royal Bavarian Professor.
Medal at Berlin.
Great Würtemberg Art Medal.
Member of the Academies of Berlin and Munich.

THE WATERING-PLACE.

16 x 9

VAUTIER (Benjamin) . . . Düsseldorf

Pupil of Jordan.
Medals, 1865–66.
Medal, Exposition Universelle, 1867.
Medal, Exposition Universelle, 1878.
Legion of Honor 1878.
Medals at Berlin.
Member of the Academies at Berlin, Munich, Antwerp, and
Amsterdam.

BOTANIST AT LUNCH.

32 x 24

121

BOUGHTON (George H.) . . London

Associate of the Royal Academy, 1879.

THE FINISHING TOUCH.

11 x 17

122

DIAZ (N.) dec'd . . . . . Paris

Medals, 1844–46–48.
Legion of Honor, 1851.
Diploma to the memory of deceased artists, Exposition Universelle,
1878.
Born, 1807. Died, 1876.

FLOWERS.

8 x 6

48

123

DAUBIGNY (C. F.) dec'd . . . **Paris**

Pupil of P. Delaroche.
Medals, 1848–53–55–57–59–67.
Legion of Honor, 1859.
Officer of the Legion of Honor, 1874.
Diploma to the memory of deceased artists, Exposition Universelle,
1878.
Born, 1817. Died, 1878.

A COOPER'S SHOP.

64 x 44

124

TROYON (Constant) dec'd . . . Paris

Pupil of Rivereux.
Medals, 1838–40–46–48–55.
Legion of Honor, 1849.
Born, 1810. Died, 1865.

THE PASTURE.

15 x 11

125

FROMENTIN (E.) dec'd . . . Paris

Pupil of Cabat.
Medals, 1849–57–59.
Legion of Honor, 1859.
Medal, Exposition Universelle, 1867.
Officer of the Legion of Honor, 1869.
Diploma to the memory of deceased artists, Exposition Universelle,
1878.
Born, 1820. Died, 1876.

TURKISH WASHER-WOMEN.

13 x 10

49

126

ROUSSEAU (Theo.) dec'd . . . **Paris**

Pupil of Lethiere.
Medals, 1834-49-55.
Legion of Honor, 1852.
One of the eight Grand Medals of Honor, Exposition Universelle,
1867.
Diploma to the memory of deceased artists, Exposition Universelle,
1878.
Born, 1812. Died, 1867.

LANDSCAPE.
11 x 8

127

BOSBOOM (Johannes) . . . Hague

Pupil of Van Bree.
Medal, Exposition Universelle, 1855.
Knight of the Order of the Lion of the Netherlands.
Knight of the Order of the Crown of Oak, and of the Order
of Leopold.
Medal, Philadelphia, 1876.

CHURCH INTERIOR.
10 x 16

128

COROT (J. B. C.) dec'd . . . Paris

Pupil of V. Bertin.
Medals, 1838-48-55.
Legion of Honor, 1846.
Medal, Exposition Universelle, 1867.
Officer of the Legion of Honor, 1867.
Diploma to the memory of deceased artists, Exposition Universelle,
1878
Born, 1796. Died, 1875.

NEAR VILLE D'AVRAY.
15 x 19

129

DUPRÉ (Jules) . . . . . **Paris**

Medal, 1833.
Legion of Honor, 1849.
Medal, Exposition Universelle, 1867.
Officer of the Legion of Honor, 1870.

DRIVING COWS TO WATER.

16 x 18

130

GALLAIT (Louis) . . . . Brussels

Medals, 1835–48.
Legion of Honor, 1841.
Chevalier of the Order of the Crown of Oak, Holland.
Honorary Member of the Royal Academy, London.
Grand Cordon of the Order of Leopold, 1881.

A YOUNG MOTHER.

8 x 10

131

ROYBET (F.) . . . . . Paris

RETURN FROM THE CHASE.

26 x 36

132

EPP (Rud.) . . . . . . Munich

SAYING GRACE.

36 x **30**

51

133

RENOUF (Emile) . . . . **Paris**

Pupil of Boulanger.
Medal, 1880.

REPAIRING THE OLD BOAT.

80 x 56

200

134

PERRAULT (Léon) . . . . **Paris**

Pupil of Bouguereau.
Medals, 1864-76.

A FLOWER-GIRL.

31 x 44

750

135

GREUTZNER (E.) . . . . Munich

THE PUZZLED PRIEST.

27 x 34

1750

136

MERLE (Hughes) dec'd . . . Paris

Pupil of Cogniet.
Medals, 1861-63.
Legion of Honor, 1866.
Born, 1822. Died, 1881.

ST. ELIZABETH OF HUNGARY.

18 x 22

52

250

137

VAN MARCKE (E.) . . . . . Paris

Pupil of Troyon.
Medals, 1867-69-70.
Legion of Honor, 1872.
First Class Medal, Exposition Universelle, 1878.

CATTLE REPOSING.
20 x 13

1800

138

SCHREYER (Ad.) . . . . . . Paris

Medals, 1864-65.
Medal, Exposition Universelle, 1867.
Vienna Exposition, 1873.

AN ARAB SCOUT.
27 x 32

1100

139

DETAILLE (E.) . . . . . **Paris**

Pupil of Meissonier.
Medals, 1869-70-72.
Legion of Honor, 1873.
Officer of the Legion of Honor, 1881.

A FRENCH LANCER.
8 x 12

500

140

BERANGER (Emile) dec'd . . . Paris

Pupil of Paul Delaroche.
Medals, 1846-48.
Born, Died, 1882.

ARRANGING FLOWERS.
9 x 12

200

5 53

METTLING (Louis) . . . . **Paris**

Pupil of the Lyons Fine Art School.

STREET SWEEPER AT LUNCH.

17 x 14

750

142

DIAZ (N.) dec'd . . . . . **Paris**

Medals, 1844-46-48.
Legion of Honor, 1851.
Diploma to the memory of deceased artists, Exposition Universelle,
1878.
Born, 1807. Died, 1876.

MOONLIGHT CONCERT.

19 x 16

2000

143

ROUSSEAU (Theo.) dec'd . . . **Paris**

Pupil of Lethiere.
Medals, 1834-49-55.
Legion of Honor, 1852.
One of the eight Grand Medals of Honor, Exposition Universelle, 1867.
Diploma to the memory of deceased artists, Exposition Universelle,
1878.
Born, 1812. Died, 1867.

A WATERFALL.

13 x 8

1500

144

RYDER (A. P.) . . . . . New-York

THE RESURRECTION.

13 x 18

350

VAN MARCKE (E.) . . . . Paris

Pupil of Troyon.
Medals, 1867–69–70.
Legion of Honor, 1872.
First Class Medal, Exposition Universelle, 1878.

THE MILL FARM.

76 x 54   *3500*

146

COROT (J. B. C.) dec'd . . . Paris

Pupil of V. Bertin.
Medals, 1838–48–55.
Legion of Honor, 1846.
Medal, Exposition Universelle, 1867.
Officer of the Legion of Honor, 1867.
Diploma to the memory of deceased artists, Exposition Universelle,
1878.
Born, 1796. Died, 1875.

LAKE NEMI.

52 x 38   *7500*

147

KAEMMERER (F. H.) . . . . Paris

Pupil of Gérôme.
Medal, 1874.

TOAST TO THE BRIDE.

42 x 29   *1500*

148

MEISSONIER (J. L. E.) . . . Paris

Pupil of Cogniet.
Medals, 1840-41-43-48.
Legion of Honor, 1846.
Grand Medal of Honor, Exposition Universelle, 1855.
Officer of the Legion of Honor, 1856.
Member of the Institute of France, 1861.
Honorary Member of the Royal Academy, London.
One of the eight Grand Medals of Honor, Exposition Universelle,
1867.
Commander of the Legion of Honor, 1867.
Grand Medal of Honor, Exposition Universelle, 1878.
Grand Officer of the Legion of Honor, 1881.

A VIDETTE, 1812.

20 x 17

149

DAGNAN-BOUVERET (P. A. J.) . Paris

Pupil of Gérôme.
Medals, 1878-80.

AN ORPHAN IN CHURCH.

21 x 17

DUPRÉ (Jules) . . . . . **Paris**

Medal, 1833.
Legion of Honor, 1849.
Medal, Exposition Universelle, 1867.
Officer of the Legion of Honor, 1870.

A SYMPHONY.

2000

39 x 27

From the collection of M. Faure.

151

DIAZ (N.) dec'd . . . . . Paris

Medals, 1844-46-48.
Legion of Honor, 1851.
Diploma to the memory of deceased artists, Exposition Universelle,
1878.
Born, 1807. Died, 1876.

GROUP OF PERSIAN WOMEN.

25 x 17 3750

152

PASSINI (L.) . . . . . Vienna

Pupil of the Academy of Vienna.
Medal, 1870.
Legion of Honor, 1878.

YOUNG GIRL OF VENICE.

Water-color.

13 x 17 500

153

CHURCH (Frederick E.)　　　　　New-York

Medal, Exposition Universelle, 1867.

"AL AYN," THE FOUNTAIN.　*750*

35 x 23

154

GÉRÔME (J. L.)　.　.　.　.　.　**Paris**

Pupil of P. Delaroche.
Medals, 1847-48.
Medal, Exposition Universelle, 1855.
Legion of Honor, 1855.
Member of the Institute of France, 1865.
Honorary Member of the Royal Academy, London.
One of the eight Grand Medals of Honor, Exposition Universelle, 1867.
Officer of the Legion of Honor, 1867.
Grand Medal of Honor, 1874.
Commander of the Legion of Honor, 1878.
Medal, Sculpture, Exposition Universelle, 1878.
Grand Medal of Honor, Exposition Universelle, 1878.
Professor in the School of the Beaux Arts.

THE *TULIP FOLLY.*

38 x 25

155

ROUSSEAU (Theo.) dec'd　.　.　.　Paris

Pupil of Lethiere.
Medals, 1834-49-55.
Legion of Honor, 1852.
One of the eight Grand Medals of Honor, Exposition Universelle, 1867.
Diploma to the memory of deceased artists, Exposition Universelle, 1878.
Born, 1812. Died, 1867.

ST. *MICHAEL'S MOUNT.*

13 x 9

156

DIAZ (N.) dec'd . . . . . Paris

Medals, 1844-46-48.
Legion of Honor, 1851.
Diploma to the memory of deceased artists, Exposition Universelle,
1878.
Born, 1807. Died, 1876.

REPOSE AFTER THE BATH.
13 x 8

1000

157

ROUSSEAU (Theo.) dec'd . . . Paris

Pupil of Lethiere.
Medals, 1834-49-55.
Legion of Honor, 1852.
One of the eight Grand Medals of Honor, Exposition Universelle, 1878
Born, 1812. Died, 1867.

A QUIET POOL.
10 x 8

1000

From the collection of Jules Lefebvre.

158

KNAUS (L.) . . . . Berlin

Pupil of the Düsseldorf Academy.
Medals, 1853-57-59.
Medal, Exposition Universelle, 1855.
Legion of Honor, 1859.
Grand Medal of Honor, Exposition Universelle, 1867.
Officer of the Legion of Honor, 1867.
Medal, Vienna, 1882.
Medal, Munich, 1883.
Professor in the Academy, Berlin.
Member of the Academies of Berlin, Vienna, Munich, Amsterdam,
Antwerp, and Christiana.
Knight of the Order of Merit.
Medals at Berlin, Weimar, etc.

A YOUNG SATYR.
10 x 8

500

BRETON (Jules) . . . . . Paris

Pupil of Devigne and Drolling.
Medals, 1855-57-59-61.
Legion of Honor, 1861.
Medal of the First Class and Officer of the Legion of Honor at the
Exposition Universelle, 1867.
Medal of Honor, Salon, 1872.
Knight of the Order of Leopold, 1881.

GOING TO THE FOUNTAIN.

11 x 16

160

MILLET (J. F.) dec'd . . . . Paris

Pupil of P. Delaroche.
Medals, 1853-64.
Medal, Exposition Universelle, 1867.
Legion of Honor, 1868.
Diploma to the memory of deceased artists, Exposition Universelle,
1878.
Born, 1814. Died, 1875.

GATHERING APPLES.

11 x 14

161

DELACROIX (Eugene) dec'd . . Paris

Pupil of Guérin.
Medals, 1824-48.
Legion of Honor, 1831.
Officer of the Legion of Honor, 1846.
Commander of the Legion of Honor, 1855.
Medal of Honor (Exposition Universelle), 1855.
Member of the Institute of France, 1857.
Born, 1798. Died, 1863.

CLEOPATRA.

13 x 10

PASINI (Albert) . . . . . Paris

Pupil of Ciceri.
Medals, 1859-63-64.
Legion of Honor, 1868.
Grand Medal of Honor (Exposition Universelle), 1878.
Officer of the Legion of Honor, 1878.

BARRACKS AT CONSTANTINOPLE.

31 x 25

1500

163

COROT (J. B. C.) dec'd . . . . Paris

Pupil of V. Bertin.
Medals, 1838-48-55.
Legion of Honor, 1846.
Medal, Exposition Universelle, 1867.
Officer of the Legion of Honor, 1867.
Diploma to the memory of deceased artists, Exposition Universelle,
1878.
Born, 1796. Died, 1875.

2500

LANDSCAPE.

31 x 21

164

DAUBIGNY (C. F.) dec'd . . . Paris

Pupil of P. Delaroche.
Medals, 1848-53-55-57-59-67.
Legion of Honor, 1859.
Officer of the Legion of Honor, 1874.
Diploma to the memory of deceased artists, Exposition Universelle,
1878.
Born, 1817. Died, 1878.

ON THE SEINE.

23 x 13

150

2500

DAUBIGNY (C. F.) dec'd . . . . Paris

Pupil of P. Delaroche.
Medals, 1848-53-55-57-59-67.
Legion of Honor, 1859.
Officer of the Legion of Honor, 1874.
Diploma to the memory of deceased artists, Exposition Universelle, 1878.
Born, 1817. Died, 1878.

ON THE MARNE.

23 x 13

VIBERT (J. G.) . . . . . Paris

Pupil of Barrias.
Medals, 1864-67-68.
Legion of Honor, 1870.
Third Class Medal, Exposition Universelle, 1878.

THE MISSIONARY'S STORY.

52 x 39

Paris Triennial Exhibition, 1883. *8000*

TROYON (C.) dec'd . . . . . Paris

Pupil of Rivereux.
Medals, 1838-40-46-55.
Legion of Honor, 1849.
Born, 1810. Died, 1865.

PASTURAGE IN NORMANDY.

33 x 24

6500

DUPRÉ (Jules) . . . . Paris

Medal, 1833.
Legion of Honor, 1849.
Medal, Exposition Universelle, 1867.
Officer of the Legion of Honor, 1870.

MORNING.

28 x 21

169

MEISSONIER (Chas.) . . . Paris

Pupil of his father.
Medal, 1866.

THE MUSICIAN.

12 x 17

170

MEYER VON BREMEN (J. G.) . Berlin

Pupil of Sohn.
Member of the Amsterdam Academy.
Gold medal of Prussia, 1850.
Medals at Berlin and Philadelphia.

THE LESSON.

10 x 14

171

DIAZ (N.) dec'd . . . . . Paris

Medals, 1844-46-48.
Legion of Honor, 1851.
Diploma to the memory of deceased artists, Exposition Universelle,
1878.
Born, 1807. Died, 1876.

A POOL IN THE WOODS.

14 x 10

172

MEYER VON BREMEN (J. G.) . Berlin

Pupil of Sohn.
Member of the Amsterdam Academy
Gold medal of Prussia, 1850.
Medals at Berlin and Philadelphia.

1500

EVENING PRAYERS.

15 x 20

173

VAN MARCKE (E.) . . . . Paris

Pupil of Troyon.
Medals, 1867-69-70.
Legion of Honor, 1872.
First Class Medal, Exposition Universelle, 1878.

GOING TO PASTURE.

39 x 26

2500

From the collection of Laurent Richard.

174

DIAZ (N.) dec'd . . . . . Paris

Medals, 1844-46-48.
Legion of Honor, 1851.
Diploma to the memory of deceased artists, Exposition Universelle,
1878.
Born, 1807. Died, 1876.

BOY WITH HUNTING-DOGS.

25 x 21

2000

MILLET (J. F.) dec'd . . . . Paris

Pupil of P. Delaroche.
Medals, 1853-64.
Medal, Exposition Universelle, 1867.
Legion of Honor, 1868.
Diploma to the memory of deceased artists, Exposition Universelle,
1878.
Born, 1814. Died, 1875.

THE CHURNER. 5000

14 x 22

Collection of Laurent Richard.

JACQUE (Charles) . . . . . Paris

Medals, 1861-63-64.
Legion of Honor, 1867.

SHEPHERDESS AND SHEEP.

17 x 23

350

CONRAD (Alb.) . . . . . Munich

THE OLD, OLD STORY.

36 x 30

65   300

BRETON (Jules) . . . . . . Paris

Pupil of Devigne and Drolling.
Medals, 1855-57-59-61.
Legion of Honor, 1861.
Medal of the First Class and Officer of the Legion of Honor at the
Exposition Universelle, 1867.
Medal of Honor, Salon, 1872.
Knight of the Order of Leopold, 1881.

RETURNING FROM THE FIELDS.

40 x 27

179

TROYON (C.) dec'd. . . . . Paris

Pupil of Rivereux.
Medals, 1838-40-46-48-55.
Legion of Honor, 1849.
Born, 1810. Died, 1865.

COAST NEAR VILLIERS.

37 x 26

180

DIAZ (N.) dec'd. . . . . . Paris

Medals, 1844-46-48.
Legion of Honor, 1851.
Diploma to the memory of deceased artists, Exposition Universelle,
1878.
Born, 1807. Died, 1876.

SUNSET AFTER A STORM.

34 x 26

BECKER (Q.) . . . . . **Berlin**

HEAD OF PEASANT WOMAN.

11 x 16

2 00

182

DIAZ (N.) dec'd. . . . . . Paris

Medals, 1844-46-48.
Legion of Honor, 1851.
Diploma to the memory of deceased artists, Exposition Universelle,
1878.
Born, 1807. Died, 1876.

ORIENTAL WOMAN.

11 x 17

1000

183

BLOMMERS (B. J.) . . . . Hague

SHOVELING SNOW.

10 x 14

500

184

HENNER (Jean J.) . . . . Paris

Pupil of Drolling and Picot.
Prize of Rome, 1858.
Medals, 1863-65-66.
Legion of Honor, 1873.
Officer of the Legion of Honor, 1878.
Medal, Exposition Universelle, 1878.

REPOSE.

36 x 27

1500

KNAUS (L.) . . . . Berlin

Pupil of the Düsseldorf Academy.
Medals, 1853–57–59.
Medal, Exposition Universelle, 1855.
Legion of Honor, 1859.
Grand Medal of Honor, Exposition Universelle, 1867.
Officer of the Legion of Honor, 1867.
Medal, Vienna, 1882.
Medal, Munich, 1883.
Professor in the Academy, Berlin.
Member of the Academies of Berlin, Vienna, Munich, Amsterdam,
Antwerp, and Christiana.
Knight of the Order of Merit.
Medals at Berlin, Weimar, etc.

THE COUNTRY STORE.
30 x 25

MILLET (J. F.) dec'd . . . . . Paris

Pupil of P. Delaroche.
Medals, 1853–64.
Medal, Exposition Universelle, 1867.
Legion of Honor, 1868.
Diploma to the memory of deceased artists, Exposition Universelle,
1878.
Born, 1814. Died, 1875.

WOOD-CUTTERS.
25 x 32

DIAZ (N.) dec'd . . . . . . Paris

Medals, 1844–46–48.
Legion of Honor, 1851.
Diploma to the memory of deceased artists, Exposition Universelle,
1878.
Born, 1807. Died, 1876.

L'ILE DES AMOURS.
24 x 16

188

DECAMPS (A. G.) dec'd . . . Paris

Pupil of Pujol.
Medals, 1831–34.
Chevalier of the Legion of Honor, 1839.
Officer of the Legion of Honor, 1851.
Born, 1803.   Died, 1860.

THE WALK TO EMMÆUS.

18 x 12

189

DIAZ (N.) dec'd . . . . Paris

Medals, 1844–46–48.
Legion of Honor, 1851.
Diploma to the memory of deceased artists, Exposition Universelle,
1878.
Born, 1807.   Died, 1876.

PERSIAN WOMAN AND CHILD.

9 x 12

6   69

BONHEUR (Rosa) Mlle. . . . Paris

Pupil of her father.
Medals, 1845-48.
Medal, Exposition Universelle, 1855.
Member of the Institute of Antwerp, 1855.
Legion of Honor, 1865.
Medal, Exposition Universelle, 1867.

DEER IN A FOREST.

31 x 39

BERNE-BELLECOUR (E. P.) . . Paris

Pupil of Picot.
Medals, 1869-72.
Legion of Honor, 1878.
Medal, Exposition Universelle, 1878.

THE LAST DROP.

5 x 6

ARTZ (Adolphe) . . . . . . Hague

Pupil of Israels.

THE FRUGAL MEAL.

51 x 37

193

FRÈRE (Éd.) . . . . Paris

Pupil of P. Delaroche.
Medals, 1851-52-55.
Legion of Honor, 1855.

PRAYER.

15 x 18

750

194

ESCOSURA (Léon y) . . . . . Paris

Pupil of Gérôme.
Commander of the Order of Isabel the Catholic.
Chevalier of the Order of Charles III. of Spain.
Chevalier of the Order of Christ, of Portugal.

CONVALESCENT PRINCE.

24 x 19

900

195

MEYER VON BREMEN (J. G.) . Berlin

Pupil of Sohn.
Member of the Amsterdam Academy.
Gold Medal of Prussia, 1850.
Medals at Berlin and Philadelphia.

DECORATING THE SHRINE.

16 x 20

750

196

HARBURGER (E.) . . . . . Munich

DUTCH PEASANT.

4 x 5

50

71

KNAUS (L.) . . . . Berlin

Pupil of the Düsseldorf Academy.
Medals, 1853–57–59.
Medal, Exposition Universelle, 1855.
Legion of Honor, 1859.
Grand Medal of Honor, Exposition Universelle, 1867.
Officer of the Legion of Honor, 1867.
Medal, Vienna, 1882.
Medal, Munich, 1883.
Professor in the Academy, Berlin.
Member of the Academies of Berlin, Vienna, Munich, Amsterdam,
Antwerp, and Christiana.
Knight of the Order of Merit.
Medals at Berlin, Weimar, etc.

ST. MARTIN'S DAY.

16 x 21

2500

198

TISSOT (J.) . . . . . London

Pupil of Leys.
Medal, 1866.

IN THE LOUVRE.

18 x 28

1000

199

TROYON (C.) dec'd . . . . Paris

Pupil of Rivereux.
Medals, 1838–40–46–48–55.
Legion of Honor, 1849.
Born, 1810. Died, 1865.

COW CHASED BY A DOG.

46 x 31

72

7500

200

MILLET (J. F.) dec'd . . . . Paris

Pupil of P. Delaroche.
Medals, 1853-64.
Medal, Exposition Universelle, 1867.
Legion of Honor, 1868.
Diploma to the memory of deceased artists, Exposition
Universelle, 1878.
Born, 1814. Died, 1875.

THE WOOL CARDER.

14 x 17

201

ROUSSEAU (Theo.) dec'd . . . Paris

Pupil of Lethiere.
Medals, 1834-49-55.
Legion of Honor, 1852.
One of the eight Grand Medals of Honor, Exposition Universelle,
1867.
Diploma to the memory of deceased artists, Exposition
Universelle, 1878.
Born, 1812. Died, 1867.

TWILIGHT.

24 x 16

202

DIAZ (N.) dec'd . . . . . Paris

Medals, 1844-46-48.
Legion of Honor, 1851.
Diploma to the memory of deceased artists, Exposition
Universelle, 1878.
Born, 1807. Died, 1876.

TOILET OF VENUS.

16 x 18

203

VIBERT (J. G.) . . . . . Paris

Pupil of Barrias.
Medals, 1864-67-68.
Legion of Honor, 1870.
Third Class Medal, Exposition Universelle, 1878

PALM-SUNDAY.

16 x 21

204

FAED (Thos.) R. A. . . . London

Pupil of the School of Design, Edinburgh.
Associate of the Royal Scottish Academy, 1849.
Member of the Royal Academy, London.

IN DOUBT.

21 x 31

205

HENNER (Jean J.) . . . . **Paris**

Pupil of Drolling and Picot.
Prize of Rome, 1858.
Medals, 1863-65-66.
Legion of Honor, 1873.
Officer of the Legion of Honor, 1878.
Medal, Exposition Universelle, 1878.

LA SOURCE.

Salon, 1881

28 x 39

206

TADEMA-ALMA (L.) R. A. . . London

Pupil of Leys.
Member of the Royal Academy, Amsterdam, **1863**.
Medal at the Salon, Paris, 1864.
Knight of the **Order of** Leopold (Belgium), 1866.
Second Class Medal **at** the International Exhibition, Paris, 1867.
Knight of the Order of the Dutch Lion, 1868.
Knight, First Class, of the Order of Merit of St. Michael, **Bavaria,**
1869.
Member of the Royal Academy of Munich, **1871.**
Knight of the Order of the Legion d'Honneur, France, **1873.**
Grand Gold Medal, Berlin, 1874.
Member of the Royal Academy of Berlin, 1875.
Member of the Society of Painters in Water-colors, London.
Knight of the Third Class, Lion d'Or of the House of Nassau, 1876.
Knight of the Third Class of the Kœnigliche Kronen-Orden of
Prussia, 1877.
Honorary Professor of the Royal Institute of Fine Arts, Naples, 1878.
First Class Medal at the International Exhibition, Paris, 1878.
Officer of the Legion of Honor, 1878.
Member of the Royal Academy, London.

ROMAN LADY FEEDING FISH.

28 x 13

207

COROT (J. B. C.) dec'd . . . . Paris

Pupil of **V.** Bertin.
Medals, 1838-48-55.
Legion of Honor, 1846.
Medal, Exposition Universelle, 1855.
Officer of the Legion of Honor, 1867.
Diploma to the memory of deceased artists, Exposition Universelle,
1878.
Born, 1796. Died, 1875.

EVENING ON A RIVER.

23 x 18

Press of Theo. L. De Vinne & Co. New-York.

www.ingramcontent.com/pod-product-compliance
Lightning Source LLC
Chambersburg PA
CBHW021528270326
41930CB00008B/1142